Journey through
NEW ORLEANS
with MERL

MERL FENNELL

FENNELL ADVENTURES

Journey Through New Orleans with Merl
Copyright © 2018 by Merl Fennell
All rights reserved. No part of this book may be reproduced or transmitted in any form or by any means without written permission from the author.

ISBN **978-1-73247-964-7**

Printed in the United States of America

Publishing info: Fennell Adventures LLC
info@fennelladventures.com
678-865-3611

How to read this book:
This is **NOT** your ordinary book! You will decide which order
your New Orleans adventure will go.
All you have to do is choose between the pages in the color **RED.**
This allows you to read this same book several times in a variety of ways.
Or
You could read this book straight through and count from 1 to 10
in English and Spanish.
If you choose this option, read each page in order.
Enjoy! 🙂

Thank you from Meri

God, for blessing us with safe travels and guidance EVERYDAY!
Jiyah, my older sister, for always looking out for me!
Jace, my older brother, I will look up to you forever!
Dad, for teaching me how to rhyme!
My mommy, Jennaye, for encouraging me to follow my dreams, to be happy, and to ALWAYS put God first in my life!

"The Lord is my strength and my shield;
my heart trusts in him, and he helps me.
My heart leaps for joy,
and with my song I praise him."

Bible verse:
Psalms 28:7 (NIV version)

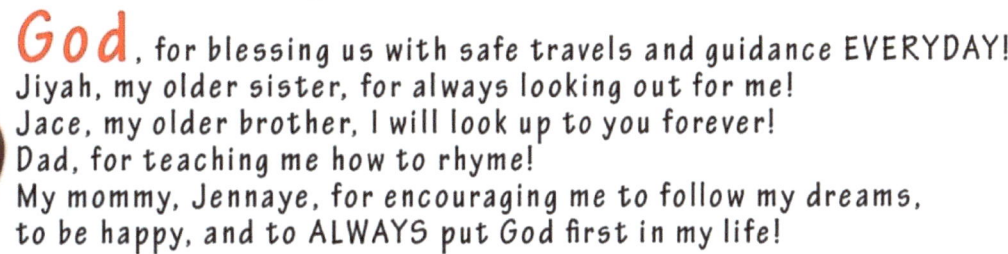

"Hey, it's me again, Merl! We are headed to New Orleans, so come on, let's begin:
"Dear God, please cover us and be our tour guide as we go on this fun family ride!"

First, let me ask you a question. Are you in a happy mood? Because it's time to learn about culture and eat some goooooood food!!

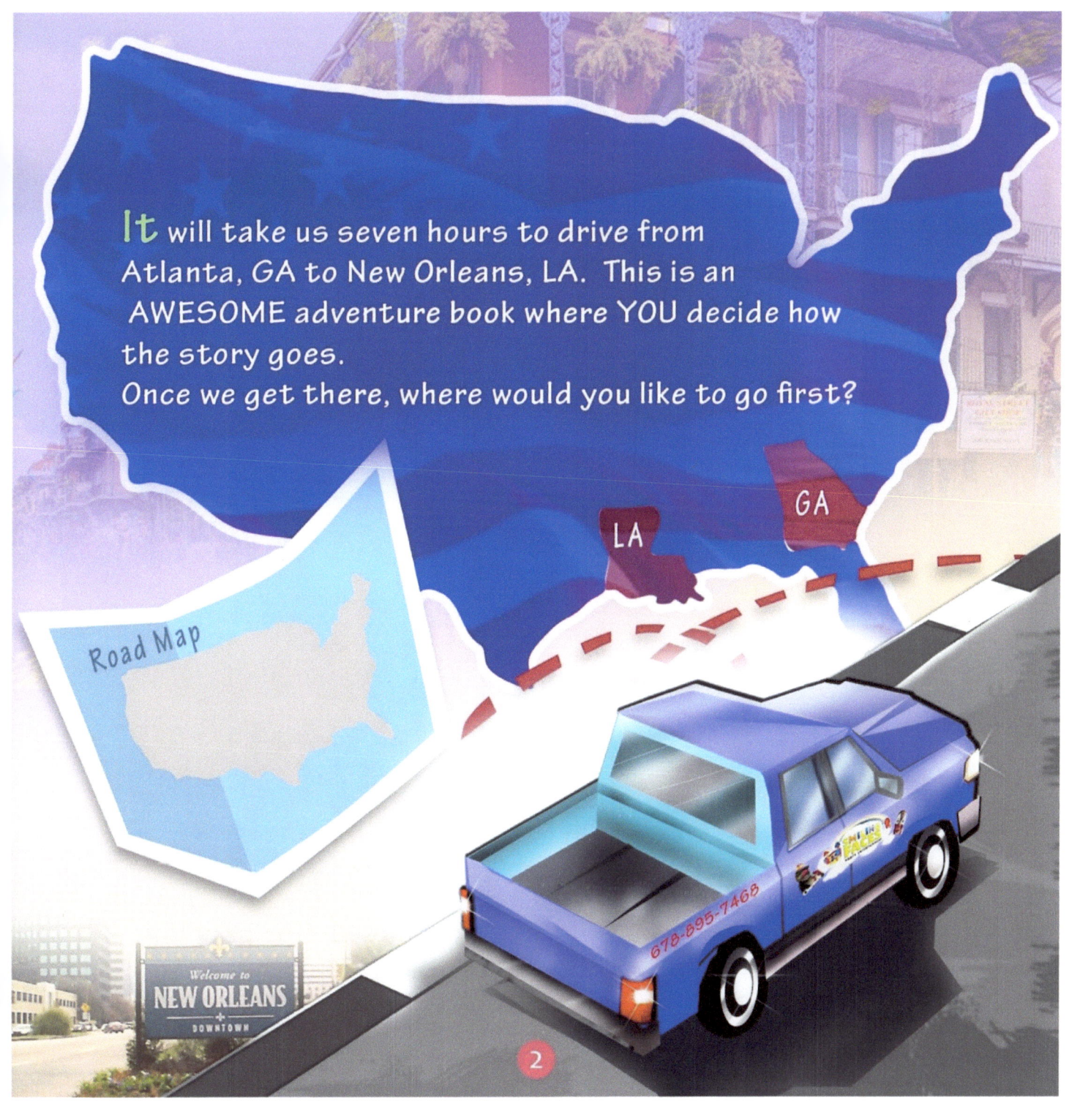

Come go with me, let's have some fun! First, we will start with the number 1!

If you would like to go swimming at the hotel pool, let's go to page 12.

If you would like to see the amazing city in a horse and buggy, let's go to page 22.

In New Orleans, there is much to do. Now, we are counting on the number 2.

If you would like to eat delicious shrimp and grits, let's go to page 18.

If you would like to end this adventure, let's go to page 23.

At Café Du Monde, they serve beignets and more. What do you know, it's the number 4!

If you would like to see where angels lay, let's go to page 16.

If you would like to end this adventure, let's go to page 23.

Fun at the pool, let's take a dive.
Look to your left, it's the number 5!

If you would like to see talented people, let's go to page 14.

If you would like to end this adventure, let's go to page 23.

On Bourbon Street, we see lots of tricks, and now we are on the number 6!

If you would like to hear instruments from a live band, let's go to page 8.

If you would like to end this adventure, let's go to page 23.

We are eating at Oceana Grill and NOLA and the food is great! On the plate is the number 8.

If you would like to see where angels lay, let's go to page 16.

If you would like to end this adventure, let's go to page 23.

We are on the airboat; look at the alligator's spine! After number 8, is the number 9!

If you would like to go swimming at the hotel pool, let's go to page 12.

If you would like to end this adventure, let's go to page 23.

The number 10 is the last of them all. On the horse and carriage ride, we are having a ball!

If you would like to eat HOT, delicious donuts called Beignets, let's go to page 10.

If you would like to see alligators from an airboat, let's go to page 20.

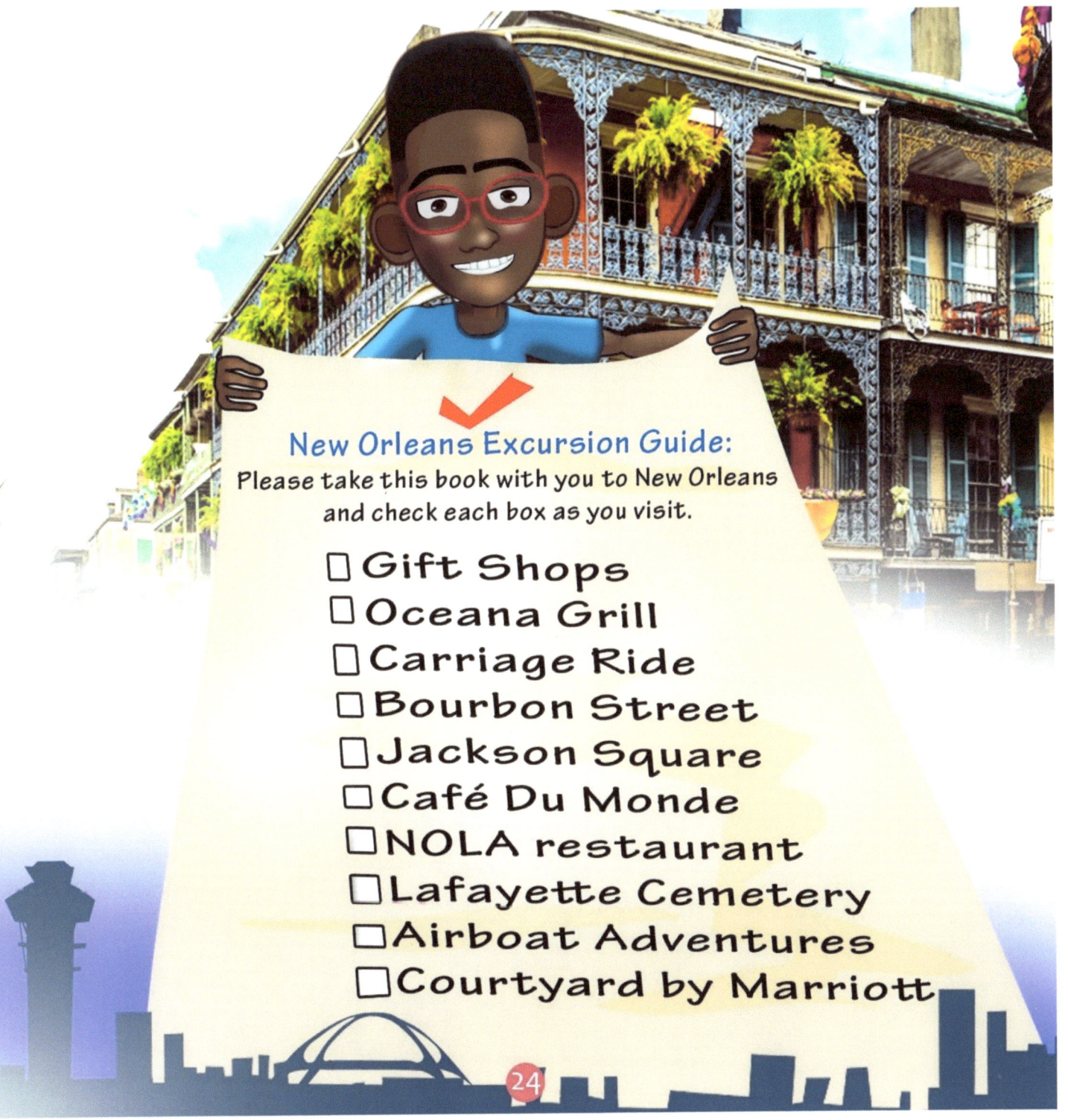

www.ingramcontent.com/pod-product-compliance
Lightning Source LLC
LaVergne TN
LVHW071030070426
835507LV00002B/98